Intro: *a note from*

Some questions nee more than once.

They hang around my life a lot of the time, by turns teasing me from the wings or challenging me centre stage. You think they've been settled and then, wow, they pop up again wearing different clothes. But underneath they're the same questions. They're the basics... things I need to wrestle with over and again as I try to make sense of a world that's at once pretty wonderful and totally confusing.

It's all to do with identity. For a start, who am I? Me. Scientific reductions lay me out on a slab in terms of chemical compounds: I'm solids, liquids, gases. Psychological babble further classifies me - defines me in terms of neuroses, hormones, primitive instincts. Relationships pin me to a family tree: I'm his sister, their mother. And social structures compartmentalise me, too. I'm his neighbour, her colleague. Stripped of all that, in essence, who am I? And, maybe more intriguing, who was I meant to be?

Accepting that I am made to be in relationship, that my life really only makes sense as it is lived out with others, leads me on to further questions of identity. As I engage with these questions it is unavoidable - if I admit that a creation demands the existence of a creator - that I look at myself in the context of some bigger plan. God, it seems, is relational, too, for why else would he have reached across the huge divide from the divine to the human by sending his Son into the world to communicate himself to me? It seems I must tackle that other big question, the one about Jesus Christ: who is he? And if I identify myself with Jesus, say I believe in him, become adopted by God and therefore joined to his family, there are issues of how I fit into that family, known as the church. What and who are the church? How does it operate as community in the 21st century, and what will belonging mean for me?

Then there is the matter of the wider world. Within my birth family there are things which make me recognisably someone who belongs. Having grown up with them, I am used to their ways, I understand their jokes, and I share identifiable genetic likeness. I have my father's hair colour, traces of a regional

Who is He? • 1

accent. And within the family of the church, though incredibly disparate, there are common basics of faith, and perhaps shared expressions of faith.

But what of the many others with whom I struggle to find a trace of common ground? I scan the faces of the people in the airport arrivals lounge. Differences. Skin colour, language, social standing, customs, educational opportunity, morality, religious conviction, political viewpoint... so many important things on which I may feel 'other' to you. Who exactly are you, when you are different to me? And how should I relate to you?

This series of four booklets attempts to tap into the wisdom of God on some of these big questions that won't go away. What does the Bible say about who I am? About who Jesus really is? About the nature of the community of believers we call the church? About who you are when you are different to me?

You won't find all the answers here. But hopefully enough to get you started on discovering for yourself.

Editor Lin Ball

GETTING THE BEST OUT OF THE IDENTITY SERIES

There are four titles in this *Bread for the Journey* series:

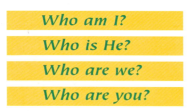

Each can be used on its own, individually or in a small group setting, or as part of a series. The material is arranged in a free-flowing way, moving between bite-sized chunks of selected Bible verses and comments.

The Bible verses are printed on the page, which makes the booklet self-contained. We've chosen the CEV (Contemporary English Version) because it's not only a translation that stands the test of good scholarship but it's readable and fresh. If you're new to Bible reading, it's a user-friendly version to begin with. If it's not a version you're familiar with, you may find it stimulating and helpful to read well-known verses put across in a new way. You can, of course, use any

Who is He? • 2

version of the Bible. You'll find the Bible references for each section given under the section headings, and Bible text is printed in italic.

The booklets are designed for reading straight through or for dipping into. You choose!

Extras: on your own or with others

It's a good idea to pray, even if it's just a couple of sentences, as you come to read. Ask God to speak to you through the material. Just the act of pausing in this way will help to focus your mind and still your heart to receive. Don't rush through the booklet. Even if you've only got a few minutes, read slowly and let the meaning sink in. If you've more time, here are a few suggestions which might make this opportunity to focus on God and his word more meaningful:

- As you read, rather than letting the words wash over you, ask yourself questions. What is this really saying? What is this showing me about God? What connection does this have with my own world, with my today?

- Keep a spiritual journal; note down things you learn about God; record fresh insights, anything you think God might be saying to you, prayer needs, answers to prayer.

- Think about how your time with God might involve some worship or expression of thankfulness. This could involve playing some praise music and singing along. Or expressing out loud your thanks to God. Or writing down your response, perhaps in a kind of 'love letter' to God.

- Listen for the voice of God! He very often chooses to speak directly to us through the Bible.

If you're part of a small fellowship group that meets weekly or fortnightly, these booklets are great for working through together. Or you might like to get some friends together over coffee for a one-off discussion. You'll find a number of questions suitable for group discussion, and some prayer ideas, too, that would work well in a group.

Most of the ideas listed here could be adapted for small group use; or in pairs within a small group. Remember that God is a God of variety. He is creative and made us to be that way too. Don't be trapped into using formats simply because that's 'the way it's always done'. Use your group's creativity and imagination. Remember to value everyone's contribution. And think about other resources that might be useful in adding width and depth to the material – for example, a current film, novel or newspaper article that explores some of the themes of identity you will find in the series.

REALITY
NEW
EVANGELISM THE MULTI-MEDIA WAY

Twelve 25 minute apologetic programmes by Michael Green

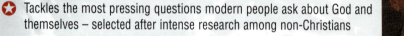 On video   On CD-Rom

★ Tackles the most pressing questions modern people ask about God and themselves – selected after intense research among non-Christians

★ Made to reach an everyday TV-audience – speaking today's language to today's people

★ Presented by author, theologian and evangelist Dr Michael Green, who guides the viewer/user through all different layers of information and answers

The 12 programmes are:
1 Who is this God? *2* Does life have any meaning? *3* Who is who in the spirit world? *4* It is not safe to die! *5* Who is this Jesus? *6* One world, one religion? *7* The good, the bad and the suffering *8* Truth, lies and videotape *9* Who is this Spirit? *10* We meant no harm *11* Can I change myself? *12* Why on earth the Church?

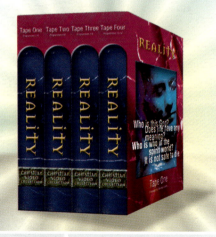

ZX367 Reality Video Course
A boxed set of four videos that look exactly like a computer running a sophisticated CD-Rom

✪ 255 page 'interactive' study guide included

Price: £60.00 + £8.00 p&p

ZX368 Reality CD-Roms
The twelve episodes on four CDs, plus...

✪ Hundreds of background articles, drama fragments and quotes from Christian and secular thinkers
✪ An integrated version of the On-Line Bible
✪ An automatic link to the Reality Internet Site
✪ Over three hundred questions
✪ Video on Demand
✪ Real Audio
✪ Web-chat and E-mail.

Price: £60.00 + £8.00 p&p

Christian Video Collection,
CPO, Garcia Estate, Canterbury Road,
Worthing, West Sussex BN13 1BW.
Tel: 01903 263354, **email**: sales@cpo.org.uk,
fax: 01903 830066;
website: www.christianvideocollection.org

TO ORDER
Call 01903 263354 (credit card orders welcomed) or send a cheque made payable to Christian Publicity Ltd at the CVC address opposite. Please quote reference number(s) above and the code CC17. Also ask for your *FREE* CVC Catalogue

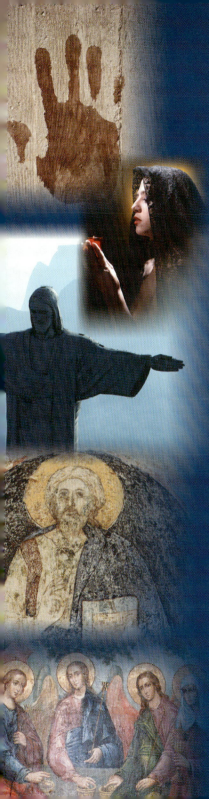

Who is he?

No DNA file.

No birth certificate.

No dental records.

No school reports.

No tax returns.

No recording of his voice.

No film footage.

No portraits.

We don't have anything he wrote or made.

But on the other hand...

He's the most famous person who's ever lived. The most debated person in history.

There are loads of films about him and libraries filled with books about him. And just about everybody has a theory about his true identity. Some people say he was no more than a good man. Others say he was a revolutionary. Or a magician. Or a con man. For some he's a mystic, a spiritual guru. For others, a myth.

Jesus: enigma

Mark 8:27-29

Jesus and his disciples went to the villages near the town of Caesarea Philippi. As they were walking along, he asked them, "What do people say about me?"

The question Jesus asked his disciples is still a key question 2000 years later.

Jesus claimed he was the source of life to the full. Sounds pretty interesting, but is it true? We need to know. He said he could give life that lasts for ever, defeating death. Promising; but can he? We need to know.

The disciples answered, "Some say you are John the Baptist or perhaps Elijah. Others say you are one of the prophets."

Then Jesus asked them, "But who do you say I am?"

Crunch point. The claims that Jesus made are so big that we can't settle for second-hand opinions. That's the challenge: read his words for yourself. Listen to the people who knew him, who were there at the time. You owe it to yourself. In asking the question, Jesus throws down the gauntlet. Now it's up to you.

Tell me...

'A man who was merely a man and said the sort of things Jesus said would not be a great moral teacher. He would either be a lunatic - on a level with the man who says he is a poached egg - or else he would be the Devil of Hell. You must make your choice. Either this man was, and is, the Son of God: or else a madman or something worse.'

Theologian C S Lewis in his book *Mere Christianity*

Jesus: promised prince

Isaiah 9:6 / Micah 5:2 / Isaiah 53:5

A child has been born for us. We have been given a son who will be our ruler. His names will be Wonderful Adviser and Mighty God, Eternal Father and Prince of Peace.

Every day *The Times* runs a page of birth announcements. With Jesus things were different. There were scores of announcements - but hundreds of years before he was born. These prophecies described the place and circumstances of his birth...

Bethlehem Ephrath, you are one of the smallest towns in the nation of Judah. But the Lord will choose one of your people to rule the nation - someone whose family goes back to ancient times.

... the purpose of his life, even the manner of his death.

He was wounded and crushed because of our sins; by taking our punishment, he made us completely well.

Jesus' entry into the world was no ordinary event. There's something seismic happening here, some huge plan reaching through centuries, unfolding...

Church of the Nativity, Bethlehem

Who is He? • 7

Jesus: world changer

Isaiah 9:7

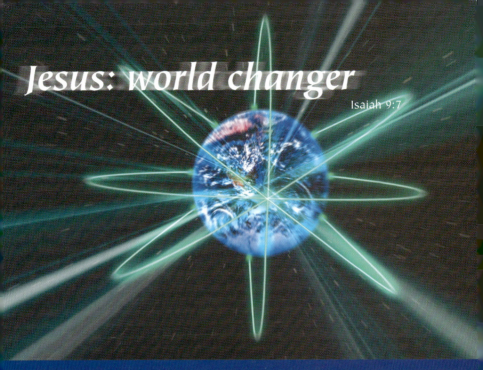

His power will never end; peace will last for ever. He will rule David's kingdom and make it grow strong. He will always rule with honesty and justice. The Lord All-Powerful will make certain that all of this is done.

We're talking total transformation: that's the agenda Jesus has. And look at the scale. This is not just some sort of personal enlightenment plan for the spiritually-minded. Changing the entire world, forever; that's the goal. The whole of time and space: that's his canvas.

In our world of suffering, injustice, brutality, insecurity, pain and confusion, this is as relevant as it gets.

THE WORD ON THE STREET

Who is He?

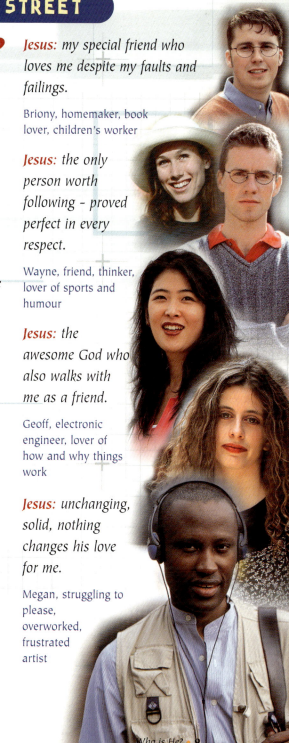

Jesus: the creator of the world, the almighty God, my saviour and my friend.

Diane, baker, watcher of golden oldie videos

Jesus: revealing himself to be powerfully in command of events that are way beyond my control at the moment, showing me every day how much he's prepared in advance for the needs of my family.

Cara, travelling mum, currently in Germany

Jesus: my Lord... but this is a jargon word. 'Boss' conveys the meaning better.

Jez, genial thirty-something new dad

Jesus: the vision for my life's purpose. His death has transformed my past, and his life inspires my future.

Ruth, teacher and nature lover

Jesus: God with skin on.

Allen, mid-career transition student and mountain-loving poet

Jesus: my only real hope for life that will last... for eternity.

David, Archers fan, working in Romania

Jesus: my special friend who loves me despite my faults and failings.

Briony, homemaker, book lover, children's worker

Jesus: the only person worth following – proved perfect in every respect.

Wayne, friend, thinker, lover of sports and humour

Jesus: the awesome God who also walks with me as a friend.

Geoff, electronic engineer, lover of how and why things work

Jesus: unchanging, solid, nothing changes his love for me.

Megan, struggling to please, overworked, frustrated artist

Jesus: shining Light

John 1:1-9

*In the beginning was the one
 who is called the Word.*

*The Word was with God
 and was truly God.*

*From the very beginning
 the Word was with God.*

*And with this Word,
 God created all things.*

*Nothing was made
 without the Word.*

*Everything that was created
 received its life from him,*

and his life gave light to everyone.

A light...

... in the darkness to find the way forward in confusion.

... to warn you of rocks ahead.

... to show you home in a cold dark place.

A light of warmth when the bitter winds blow.

*The light keeps shining
 in the dark,
 and darkness has never
 put it out.*

A light that...

... sets the past aflame and gives a new start.

... reveals things as they truly are.

A light of dawning hope, of understanding.

*God sent a man named John,
 who came to tell
 about the light*

*and to lead all people
 to have faith.*

John wasn't that light.

*He came only to tell
 about the light.*

*The true light that shines
 on everyone
 was coming into the world.*

Jesus, the light. **What sort of light do you need now?** Ask him, not just to be the light, but to be your light.

Who is He? • 10

Jesus: breaker of rules

Luke 1:26-35, 38 / Luke 2:5-7

God sent the angel Gabriel to the town of Nazareth in Galilee with a message for a virgin named Mary. She was engaged to Joseph from the family of King David.

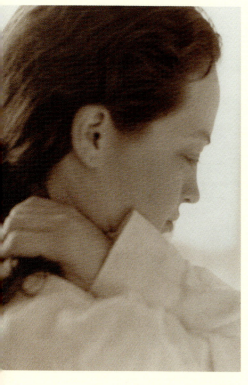

The angel greeted Mary and said, "You are truly blessed! The Lord is with you."

Mary was confused by the angel's words and wondered what they meant. Then the angel told Mary, "Don't be afraid! God is pleased with you, and you will have a son. His name will be Jesus. He will be great and will be called the Son of God Most High. The Lord God will make him king, as his ancestor David was. He will rule the people of Israel for ever, and his kingdom will never end."

Mary asked the angel, "How can this happen? I am not married!"

The angel answered, "The Holy Spirit will come down to you, and God's power will come over you. So your child will be called the holy Son of God."

Mary and her parents around the dinner table. Awkward silences. Always such a sensible girl... now look at her, eyes down, trying to cover up with this ridiculous story about an angel. So looking forward

Who is He? • 11

to her wedding, and then the doting grandparents' routine. Then this. Only a teenager. The boyfriend unsure what to do. Neighbours glance, then look away.

It's as though Jesus went out of his way to arrive on planet earth in the most unceremonious way possible. Obscurity, confusion, embarrassment. Jesus doesn't work by our rules. He constantly throws us off balance. Mary found the best way to handle this: accept and trust.

Mary said, "I am the Lord's servant! Let it happen as you have said." And the angel left her.

Picture it. A huge celebrity launch with film stars and politicians paying thousands of pounds for the tickets, the jostling photographers of the world's press, simultaneous broadcasts by satellite, live-linked across the globe through the Internet. That's how God could have announced his arrival. Get everyone's attention, make people sit up and take notice. But no.

Mary was engaged to Joseph and travelled with him to Bethlehem. She was soon going to have a baby, and while they were there, she gave birth to her firstborn son. She dressed him in baby clothes and laid him on a bed of hay, because there was no room for them in the inn.

Instead, he arrives 1500 years before the printing press is invented. Instead of the big city, he arrives in a tiny hamlet. The parents: beautiful people on the cover of *Hello?* Actually, a couple of ordinary but godly people. Instead of a massive fireworks display, angels perform to a handful of sleepy shepherds. Instead of a hospital with all the latest equipment, it's an animal shed and a first night in a feeding trough. What would the health visitor say? Social Services would probably call them unsuitable parents and take the baby away. And in just a few weeks, he'll be hunted, fleeing the country, a refugee before he can even control his bladder. And this is just the start. Jesus always has the capacity to shock, to offend. He dares to challenge our preconceptions.

Jesus: ready for the road

Mark 1:1-5, 7-11

This is the good news about Jesus Christ, the Son of God. It began just as God had said in the book written by Isaiah the prophet,

"I am sending my messenger to get the way ready for you.

In the desert someone is shouting,

'Get the road ready for the Lord!

Make a straight path for him.' "

So John the Baptist appeared in the desert and told everyone, "Turn back to God and be baptized! Then your sins will be forgiven."

From all Judea and Jerusalem crowds of people went to John. They told how sorry they were for their sins, and he baptized them in the River Jordan.

John also told the people, "Someone more powerful is going to come. And I am not good enough even to stoop down and untie his sandals. I baptize you with water, but he will baptize you with the Holy Spirit!"

About that time Jesus came from Nazareth in Galilee, and John baptized him in the River Jordan. As soon as Jesus came out of the water, he saw the sky open and the Holy Spirit coming down to him like a dove. A voice from heaven said, "You are my own dear Son, and I am pleased with you."

A glimpse of mystery. The Bible says that there is only one God. But this one God is not some abstract force; God has three persons; the Father, the Son (Jesus) and the Holy Spirit. Jesus is commissioned for his task. The Holy Spirit comes to him; the Father declares his pleasure. We see intimacy, love, union. We see that God is happy, that he celebrates. God wants all of us to experience his extraordinary love and joy, to be restored as his family. That's why Jesus came. God wants his kids back.

Who is He? • 13

Jesus: tough cookie

Matthew 4:1-11

The Holy Spirit led Jesus into the desert, so that the devil could test him. After Jesus had gone without eating for forty days and nights, he was very hungry.

Forget wimp. The desert: blistering heat by day. As cold as a meat locker at night. How well do you sleep, my friend, when you're cold and hungry? Forty days. No food, no water. And then the devil himself turns up.

Then the devil came to him and said, "If you are God's Son, tell these stones to turn into bread."

Showdown. Heavyweights division. Satan, typically, starts by throwing one below the belt: freshly baked bread, the warm smell wafting...

Jesus answered, "The Scriptures say: 'No one can live only on food. People need every word that God has spoken.'"

No messing. A complete stopper. Not even a flinch. Round 1 to Jesus.

Next, the devil took Jesus to the holy city and made him stand on the highest part of the temple. The devil said, "If you are God's Son, jump off. The Scriptures say:

'God will give his angels
    orders about you.
They will catch you
    in their arms,
and you won't hurt
    your feet on the stones."'

Cleverer now, learned his lesson, quoting scripture this time...

Jesus answered, "The Scriptures also say, 'Don't try to test the Lord your God!'"

Not fooled for a second. Saw it coming, ready for it. Round 2 to Jesus.

Finally, the devil took Jesus up on a very high mountain and showed him all the kingdoms on earth and their power. The devil said to him, "I will give all this to you, if you will bow down and worship me."

The big one. He is a king after all. Why not take the short cut?

Jesus answered, "Go away Satan! The Scriptures say:

'Worship the Lord your God
    and serve only him."'

Like hitting a brick wall. Except that this one hits back like a steam shovel. Round 3 to Jesus. The Devil calls for time out.

Then the devil left Jesus, and angels came to help him.

The battle will go on but, in the end, only one will be left standing. Jesus will be criticised, misunderstood, rejected, and betrayed. But not even once does he give way to a single selfish thought, word or action. He lives a perfect, flawless life. Jesus: a tough cookie. You've got to respect that sort of strength.

Who is He? • 15

Jesus: bringer of good news

Matthew 4:23-25 / Mark 1:17,18

Jesus went all over Galilee, teaching in the Jewish meeting places and preaching the good news about God's kingdom. He also healed every kind of disease and sickness.

News about him spread all over Syria, and people with every kind of sickness or disease were brought to him. Some of them had a lot of demons in them, others were thought to be mad, and still others could not walk. But Jesus healed them all.

Large crowds followed Jesus from Galilee and the region around the ten cities known as Decapolis. They also came from Jerusalem, Judea, and from across the River Jordan.

Maybe it's the worst charge we can make against the church; that it has made Jesus' message boring, unattractive, irrelevant. Jesus' message was good news! People flocked to hear it, they missed work, walked for miles, skipped meals, crammed into houses, climbed trees to hear it. If we're not excited by the message it can only mean we haven't understood it yet.

It's a message about a totally different kind of community, on earth and continuing after death, a new kingdom - and how to enter it. It's a message about people: not buildings, institutions, hierarchies, formulas, systems, organisations, models or methods. People. God's love for them.

Jesus said to them, "Come with me! I will teach you how to bring in people instead of fish." At once the two brothers dropped their nets and went with him.

People dropped everything to follow Jesus: that's the imperative of the Kingdom. Has the good news of the Kingdom gripped you? What would you drop everything for? Or are you holding so tightly to stuff that you're not ready to move when he calls?

Who is He? • 16

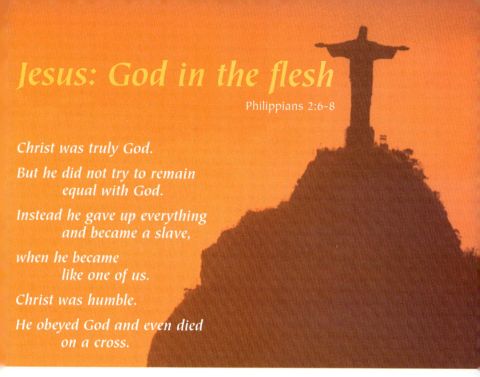

Jesus: God in the flesh

Philippians 2:6-8

Christ was truly God.
But he did not try to remain
    equal with God.
Instead he gave up everything
    and became a slave,
when he became
    like one of us.
Christ was humble.
He obeyed God and even died
    on a cross.

Jesus' mission is big: to reconcile humanity to God; to break the power of sin; to destroy the strangleholds of injustice, suffering and fear; to conquer death and defeat the devil.

To accomplish this he leaves behind his cosmic power, stays the armies of angels, and takes on human form. Not the human form of films and storybooks - tall, blond, handsome, with billowing white robes. Real humanity: born through a birth canal; filling nappies; strong rough hands from years of carpentry; yawning in the evenings, damp patches under his arms after a long day preaching, thirsty after a long walk.

Yes, the Lord of creation tied himself to one place at one time, to the limitations of a frail human body. A tiny figure on the twilight hilltop, he sets out to change the history of the universe.

Tell me...

Jesus is: 'the self-expression of the Father - what the Father has to say.'

Theologian C S Lewis in his book *Mere Christianity*

If Jesus Christ is not true God, how could he help us? If he is not true man, how could he help us?'

Twentieth century Christian martyr Dietrich Bonhoeffer

'Gentle Jesus, meek and mild is a snivelling modern invention, with no warrant in the Gospels.'

Writer George Bernard Shaw

Who is He? • 17

Jesus: healer

Mark 1:30-34 / Mark 1:42-44

...Jesus was told that Simon's mother-in-law was sick in bed with fever. Jesus went to her. He took hold of her hand and helped her up. The fever left her, and she served them a meal.

That evening after sunset, all who were si[ck] or had demons in them were brought to Jesus. In fact, the whole town gathered around the door of the house. Jesus heale[d] all kinds of terrible diseases and forced ou[t] a lot of demons

'**If only Jesus** would heal my friend, so that I could really see something, then I'd believe.' How often have we heard something like that, or said it ourselves?

Yes, Jesus healed many people. But what's interesting is that he often told people to keep it quiet.

At once the man's leprosy disappeared, and he was well.

After Jesus strictly warned the man, he sent him on his way. He said, "Don'[t] tell anyone about this."

Jesus healed so many people - and still does today - yet he often seemed to downplay these amazing things. Why? Well, for a start it wasn't the primary goal of his mission. Healed people would one d[ay] die again. Jesus was in the business of changing people for ever. He wanted people not just to have a repaired body, but to be spiritual[ly] reborn so that they would live eternally, with God.

And many people who saw extraordinary healings take place still did not believe. Sometimes they were sceptical, sometimes critical.

Who is He?

Jesus: miracle worker

Mark 6:34-44 / John 6:14,15 / Mark 1:41 / Mark 14:7

When Jesus got out of the boat, he saw the large crowd that was like sheep without a shepherd. He felt sorry for the people and started teaching them many things.

That evening the disciples came to Jesus and said, "This place is like a desert, and it is already late. Let the crowds leave, so they can go to the farms and villages near here and buy something to eat."

Jesus replied, "You give them something to eat."

But they asked him, "Don't you know that it would take almost a year's wages to buy all these people something to eat?"

Then Jesus said, "How much bread do you have? Go and see!"

They found out and answered, "We have five small loaves of bread and two fish."

Jesus told his disciples to make the people sit down on the green grass. They sat down in groups of a hundred and groups of fifty.

Jesus took the five loaves and the two fish. He looked up towards heaven and blessed the food. Then he broke the bread and handed it to his disciples to give to the people. He also divided the two fish, so that everyone could have some.

After everyone had eaten all they wanted, Jesus' disciples picked up twelve large baskets of leftover bread and fish.

There were five thousand men who ate the food.

Jesus performed a number of miracles, such as feeding the five thousand. But why not a lot more? And why so often when people demanded a miracle, did he refuse?

Miracles certainly attracted a crowd. But Jesus didn't want a fan club. He didn't want people just chasing a roadshow. He didn't want people trying to force him to work their way, by making him a king.

After the people had seen Jesus perform this miracle, they began saying, "This must be the Prophet who is to come into the world!" Jesus realized that they would try to force him to be their king. So he went up on a mountain, where he could be alone.

He would not be forced into their mould. His agenda was to bring people to genuine sorrow for their wrongdoing and a desire for a new direction, to faith in him, to new life, to obedience to God's ways. Miracles only occasionally helped: very often people were sceptical, sometimes they were critical, often they just plain missed the point. So why did Jesus perform miracles at all? Certainly out of compassion.

Jesus felt sorry for the man. So he put his hand on him and said, "... Now you are well."

Jesus cared for people so much that he loved to respond to their needs. Whether they deserved it or not. And yes, as a sign, a pointer to those who were looking with the eyes of faith. A sign showing that the coming kingdom is a place of healing, wholeness and wonder. Miracles: a glimpse into the heart of God; and a foretaste, a glimmer of a wonderful future breaking into the subnormal present.

Jesus has given us the opportunity to be like him, to love people as he does. Who and what are you compassionate about?

You will always have the poor with you. And whenever you want to, you can give to them.

<u>Lord, please teach me to love like you</u>. Teach me to face the uncomfortable feelings, the risks of reaching out to others as you did. Please change me. You've called us to carry on your work, to make you known across the earth. Help me to be Jesus-on-my-street.

Jesus: friend of those who get it wrong
Mark 2:13-17

...Jesus went to the shore of Lake Galilee. A large crowd gathered around him, and he taught them. As he walked along, he saw Levi, the son of Alphaeus. Levi was sitting at the place for paying taxes, and Jesus said to him, "Come with me!" So he got up and went with Jesus.

Later, Jesus and his disciples were having dinner at Levi's house. Many tax collectors and other sinners had become followers of Jesus, and they were also guests at the dinner.

Some of the teachers of the Law of Moses were Pharisees, and they saw that Jesus was eating with sinners and tax collectors. So they asked his disciples, "Why does he eat with tax collectors and sinners?"

Who is He? • 21

Jesus heard them and answered, "Healthy people don't need a doctor, but sick people do. I didn't come to invite good people to be my followers. I came to invite sinners."

In Jesus' day there were a whole heap of no-go areas; things you didn't do, people you weren't to be seen with. Jesus ploughed right across every boundary. He shocked everybody. He spent time with all the outsiders: prostitutes, tax-collectors, lepers, Samaritans. He talked with Romans, the occupying forces. He risked his reputation as a teacher by talking to women, and playing with children. He went to parties, associated with dangerous revolutionaries. He never said things just to please people, to get popular. He was always his own man.

All these people had probably disqualified themselves in their own eyes. None of them would have expected Jesus to turn his face towards them, to show them kindness.

Lord, sometimes I feel that I've disqualified myself from your love. There's things I've done, thoughts I regret; my faith seems so weak, my prayers so rare; I see so much selfishness in me. I'm not good enough. But you came for the not-good-enoughs of this world. You are the friend of the disqualified. You welcome me into your presence.

Jesus: master swordsman

Matthew 21:23-27

We all love to see a good interview on TV. To see Robin Day or Jeremy Paxman locking horns with a politician trying to get the upper hand.

The Pharisees thought they were pretty hot interviewers, thought they could get Jesus on the spot, catch him out, blow his credibility, make him look foolish. Let's see how they get on....

Jesus had gone into the temple and was teaching when the chief priests and the leaders of the people came up to him. They asked, "What right do you have to do these things? Who gave you this authority?"

Who is He? • 22

Jesus answered, "I have just one question to ask you. If you answer it, I will tell you where I got the right to do these things. Who gave John the right to baptize? Was it God in heaven or merely some human being?"

They thought it over and said to each other, "We can't say that God gave John this right. Jesus will ask us why we didn't believe John. On the other hand, these people think that John was a prophet, and we are afraid of what they might do to us. That's why we can't say that it was merely some human who gave John the right to baptize." So they told Jesus, "We don't know."

Jesus said, "Then I won't tell you who gave me the right to do what I do."

The tables turned: the Pharisees speechless! Check out Matthew 22:15-22 for another example of his swordplay.

Jesus: radical teacher

Luke 6:20-22,27-36

Jesus looked at his disciples and said:

"God will bless you people who are poor.

> His kingdom belongs to you!

God will bless

> you hungry people.

You will have plenty

> to eat!

God will bless you people who are crying.

> You will laugh!"

God will bless you when others hate you and won't have anything to do with you. God will bless you when people insult you and say cruel things about you, all because you are a follower of the Son of Man.

This is what I say to all who will listen to me:

"Love your enemies, and be good to everyone who hates you. Ask God to bless anyone who curses you, and pray for everyone who is cruel to you. If someone slaps you on one cheek, don't stop that person from slapping you on the other cheek. If someone wants to take your coat, don't try to keep back your shirt. Give to everyone who asks and don't ask people to return what they have taken from you. Treat others just as you want to be treated.

If you love only someone who loves you, will God praise you for that? Even sinners love people who love them. If you are kind only to someone who is kind to you, will God be pleased with you for that?

Even sinners are kind to people who are kind to them. If you lend money only to someone you think will pay you back, will God be pleased with you for that? Even sinners lend to sinners because they think they will get it all back.

Who is He? • 24

But love your enemies and be good to them. Lend without expecting to be paid back. Then you will get a great reward, and you will be the true children of God in heaven. He is good even to people who are unthankful and cruel. Have pity on others, just as your Father has pity on you."

These days everyone's into 'personal empowerment', getting our 'rights'. But Jesus says God favours the powerless. People look for prestige and status. Jesus says we should go for humility and meekness. We live in a materialist culture. Jesus says that God's heart is for the poor. Everybody wants to be top dog. Jesus tells us to love our enemies.

Jesus' teaching isn't about fine-tuning our lives to become more successful or a better person. It challenges everything: our values, our culture, our beliefs and behaviour.

Jesus is actually showing us another world, the real world. This world is only a shadowy reflection of the real world. Living in the real world is how we live life to the full. Living in the real world is about living God-centred and living by God's power. That's the only way it can work. Jesus challenges us to come out of our shadow world, to see things the right way around.

Take a hard look at your values. What are you aiming for in life? What are your priorities? Are they the stuff of this world, or of the real world?

Who is He? • 25

Author Interview

Meet our writer Chris

Chris is a Yorkshireman by birth, spent some time in Lancashire, but most of his growing up happened in a beautiful Derbyshire village which he still misses.

From the local comprehensive he moved on to a history degree at Cambridge, which is where - to his astonishment! - he became a Christian.

Chris moved to London in 1981, joined a local church and has been there ever since - quite unusual for an inner city church. For eight years he worked for the National Audit Office, something he 'hugely enjoyed', and then gave that up to become assistant minister at his church and, in time, the minister.

'The church I lead is small, but wonderful!' says Chris. 'The people are a real mixture: African, West Indian, Filipino, Indian, American, New Zealander, Australian; a good spread of ages, all personality types and walks of life - we even have a rocket scientist! There's a tremendous family atmosphere, but it's not introverted or cosy: there's a genuine desire to reach out to other people, both in evangelism and care for the poor.'

Chris loves family life with his wife Charlotte and their three young kids. In his 'spare' time he's a volunteer for a telephone helpline - 'demanding but very worthwhile', he says. For relaxation, he chooses cycling, reading a good book, or blasting alien invaders on his computer.

Chris, did you have any misconceptions about Jesus before you were a Christian?

I mostly thought of Jesus as being a good man, but nothing more. I'd been to Sunday School and to a teenagers' Pathfinder group, and I guess that this was the picture that mostly communicated, or at least it's what I picked up!

When I became a Christian, it was essentially because I encountered the Jesus who was crucified and resurrected: not just a good man, not just one of the many routes to God, but God himself! Wow!

How has your personal picture of Jesus developed over the years?

Who is He?

Well, I'm not sure developed is the word: 'exploded' is more what comes to mind! Jesus is so much bigger than all my preconceptions; even the ones I didn't know I had keep getting shattered! I'm amazed at how radical Jesus is: his strategy for how life is to be lived is so extraordinary. It really does turn the world's values upside down - or right way up?

Were there any aspects of Jesus' character that particularly challenged you as you were writing?

I was struck again with just how 'in yer face' Jesus could be! His dealings with the religious leaders, and his encounters with Satan show how combative he could be! And yet at the same time he was incredibly compassionate and caring towards vulnerable people. It's challenged me a great deal. Maybe I should be less polite and middle-class: perhaps I need to take more emotional risks in loving people, and be willing to be a bit more abrasive when it comes to defending the needs of the poor, standing up for truth and justice. Oh, dear!

What is the most important aspect of his personality to you right now?

I'm gripped by how balanced and complete a person Jesus is. And I don't mean the balance that comes from being safely in the middle, a bit of this and a bit of that in a nice compromise. Everything about him is right at the far edge, so it's a balance that's completely radical, that covers the whole ground. He's completely committed to the Father; and wholly given to people; he's an undoubted man of action... who spends huge amounts of time in prayer; he can scare the pants off everybody in authority... and yet make kids and outcasts feel welcome. Do you see what I'm getting at?

> I was struck again with just how 'in yer face' Jesus could be!

What myths do you think society holds about Jesus?

Our society has all sorts of different ideas about Jesus, of course. What they pretty much all have in common is that they take just the 'edited highlights'. They focus on the bits that fit in with whatever makes us comfortable. We want to tame Jesus, make him safe, make him fit in with our ideas. These myths - Jesus the good man, Jesus the New Age guru, and so on - are damaging because they get in the way of an encounter with the real Jesus, an encounter that would gloriously transform our lives, an encounter that would kill us, and make us unkillable.

Jesus is a Lion. You might think you've got him safely caged. You haven't. He's on the loose.

Who is He? • 27

Jesus: story teller

Matthew 13:3-9

Then he taught them many things by using stories.

He said:

"A farmer went out to scatter seed in a field. While the farmer was scattering the seed, some of it fell along the road and was eaten by birds. Other seeds fell on thin, rocky ground and quickly started growing because the soil wasn't very deep. But when the sun came up, the plants were scorched and dried up, because they did not have enough roots. Some other seeds fell where thorn bushes grew up and choked the plants. But a few seeds did fall on good ground where the plants produced a hundred or sixty or thirty times as much as was scattered. If you have ears, pay attention!"

Just imagine it... 'Even after all these years, I can still remember that afternoon with Jesus, the things he said. You know, I must have sat through hundreds of sermons in the synagogue, and I can't remember any of them. And the number of soundbites and glib one-liners from politicians, well, they're beyond counting, and long since turned to dust! But Jesus had this way of telling stories. Just everyday situations. Easy to connect to, easy to carry around in your mind. But not bedtime stories for kids. No, his stories made you work. He had this way of throwing you off balance to make you think again. Sometimes he'd say the craziest things and people would laugh, and then you'd see the laughter die, and the cogs start turning. Sometimes it was like a puzzle, so that the more you thought about it, the more the truth kept growing inside of you. Amazing really.'

> Why not read some more of the parables? Try the rest of Matthew 13 for starters.

Jesus doesn't want to spoon feed us. Truth is not fast food. It's steak. For chewing. Following Jesus isn't armchairs and isn't academic: it's action.

THE WORD ON THE STREET

Who is He?

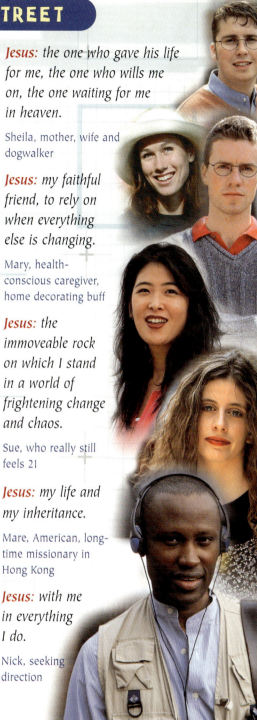

Jesus: the son of God who came to save me from my sin and restore my friendship with God.

Eileen, hill-walking clinical scientist

Jesus: the person who has brought meaning, purpose and value into life.

Colin, world traveller

Jesus: the constant in the middle of change.

Eleanor, chocaholic cross-stitcher

Jesus: my best friend, he's always with me, he never lets me down, I can talk to him whenever I want, and he's helping me through each day.

Neil, who in his dreams wins the Tour de France!

Jesus: my risen saviour, which convinces me that in him I, too, can overcome all things.

John, sports fan, world politics consumer, mission fanatic

Jesus: my rescuer, the lifter of my burdens.

Lynne, who wants to see others rescued

Jesus: the one who gave his life for me, the one who wills me on, the one waiting for me in heaven.

Sheila, mother, wife and dogwalker

Jesus: my faithful friend, to rely on when everything else is changing.

Mary, health-conscious caregiver, home decorating buff

Jesus: the immoveable rock on which I stand in a world of frightening change and chaos.

Sue, who really still feels 21

Jesus: my life and my inheritance.

Mare, American, long-time missionary in Hong Kong

Jesus: with me in everything I do.

Nick, seeking direction

Who is He? • 29

Jesus: giver of good gifts

Matthew 7:7,8;11 / Matthew 6:8

Ask, and you will receive. Search, and you will find. Knock, and the door will be opened for you. Everyone who asks will receive. Everyone who searches will find. And the door will be opened for everyone who knocks.

As bad as you are, you still know how to give good gifts to your children. But your heavenly Father is even more ready to give good things to people who ask.

God isn't some divine butler, just there to meet all our needs, to indulge us. It's the other way around: we're here to glorify him. But Jesus loves to respond to us, to provide for us. We can go to him freely and ask.

Your Father knows what you need before you ask.

He knows how to meet your needs in the way that ultimately is best for you. <u>Why not bring your needs and concerns to him now?</u> You don't have to use special words when you pray. Just talk to him. And talk to him about the needs of other people you know.

Jesus: revolutionary

Matthew 26:51-53 / John 3:3-5 / Ezekiel 36:26,27

There are revolutionaries of every sort - political, social, scientific, religious. They try to change governments, systems, ideas, institutions. Ultimately Jesus overturns the lot! But Jesus doesn't work the way the world does. For a start, he doesn't use physical force and violence.

One of Jesus' followers pulled out a sword. He struck the servant of the high priest and cut off his ear.

But Jesus told him, "Put your sword away. Anyone who lives by fighting will die by fighting. Don't you know that I could ask my Father, and straight away he would send me more than twelve armies of angels?"

He uses different weapons, far more powerful: love, sacrifice, humility, serving, forgiveness. It takes a lot of courage to change the world this way.

And then again, he's not content to change the external things alone. In fact Jesus is a revolutionary of the most radical kind, the most dangerous of all. He changes people, changes lives. In fact it's about a completely new start...

Who is He? • 31

Jesus replied, "I tell you for certain that you must be born from above before you can see God's kingdom!"

Nicodemus asked, "How can a grown man ever be born a second time?"

Jesus answered:

"I tell you for certain that before you can get into God's kingdom, you must be born not only by water, but by the Spirit."

...And a completely new heart. This is how God promised that through the Old Testament prophet Ezekiel:

I will take away your stubborn heart and give you a new heart and a desire to be faithful. You will have only pure thoughts, because I will put my Spirit in you and make you eager to obey my laws and teachings.

He gets right inside. Where there's no hiding, no escape. He wants to change your life. Completely.

Ask God for a new start and a new heart. If he has already been at work, changing you, thank him and ask him to continue to make you more like Jesus. More like the person you were meant to be.

And once right inside us, he revolutionises our priorities.

Perhaps your top priority is your career, and it's taking over the rest of your life. You've heard it before. No one ever said on their death bed: "If only I'd spent more time in the office..." Jesus challenges our priorities. What's important in your life? What do you give your time and energies to? Will you look back with regret, for missed opportunities? Not when you make his kingdom your goal.

Jesus: crucified!
Mark 15:22-39

The soldiers took Jesus to Golgotha, which means "Place of a Skull". There they gave him some wine mixed with a drug to ease the pain, but he refused to drink it.

They nailed Jesus to a cross and gambled to see who would get his clothes. It was about nine o'clock in the morning when they nailed him to the cross. On it was a sign that told why he was nailed there. It read, "This is the King of the Jews." The soldiers also nailed two criminals on crosses, one to the right of Jesus and the other to his left.

People who passed by said terrible things about Jesus. They shook their heads and shouted, "Ha! So you're the one who claimed you could tear down the temple and build it again in three days. Save yourself and come down from the cross!"

The chief priests and the teachers of the Law of Moses also made fun of Jesus. They said to each other, "He saved others, but he can't save himself. If he is the Messiah, the king of Israel, let him come down from the cross! Then we will see and believe." The two criminals also said cruel things to Jesus.

About midday the sky turned dark and stayed that way until around three o'clock. Then about that time Jesus shouted, "Eloi, Eloi, lema sabachthani?" which means, "My God, my God, why have you deserted me?"

Some of the people standing there heard Jesus and said, "He is calling for Elijah." One of them ran and grabbed a sponge. After he had soaked it in wine, he put it on a stick and held it up to Jesus. He said, "Let's wait and see if Elijah will come and take him down!" Jesus shouted and then died.

At once the curtain in the temple tore in two from top to bottom.

A Roman army officer was standing in front of Jesus. When the officer saw how Jesus died, he said, "This man really was the Son of God!"

Weird biographies, the Gospels. No physical description of Jesus. Forget the films and the Sunday school pictures: we have no idea what he looked like, none at all. Virtually nothing about his formative childhood days, no stories of his teenage years. No psychological profile. We get accounts that sweep through three extraordinary years of his life, and then suddenly the focus changes. The camera zooms in. Time slows down. We get a moment by moment and literally a blow by blow account of the hours leading up to his death. Because this is the storm-centre, the climax of his mission. Not just a good man teaching us to be nice to one another. But to die. To die in place of every human being who has ever lived. To die in order to cancel out every selfish thought and action. To die so that people could be restored to God. To die for you.

Jesus, you were prepared to go through your mission not in splendour and fame, but in torture, isolation, pain, humiliation, blood and death. That's what it took to open up a way for people to be re-connected with God. That's the measure of your love. It cost. Thank you.

Jesus: saviour

John 3:16,17

God loved the people of this world so much that he gave his only Son, so that everyone who has faith in him will have eternal life and never really die. God did not send his Son into the world to condemn its people. He sent him to save them!

Saved from what ?
The selfishness that separates us from God, cuts us off from our purpose, and from power. The selfishness that is destructive, like acid eating us away on the inside. The selfishness that makes us a slave to Satan and death.

Saved for what ?
For life as it's meant to be, God-centred, power-filled, purposeful, whole and celebratory! Life forgiven. Life to the full. Life forever.

Jesus: bread for the journey

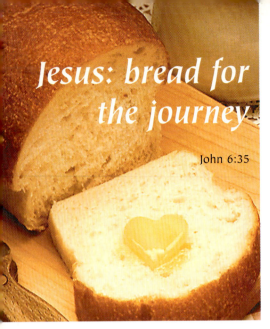

John 6:35

I am the bread that gives life! No one who comes to me will ever be hungry. No one who has faith in me will ever be thirsty.

Who is Jesus to you?

Jesus is given a number of wonderful titles in the Bible. Good shepherd, for example. Bread of life. King of kings. The true vine. They're worth exploring, thinking about in terms of your perception of him, when you've a few minutes to spare and a Bible to hand.

Jesus: risen from the dead

Luke 24:1-3

Very early on Sunday morning the women went to the tomb, carrying the spices that they had prepared. When they found the stone rolled away from the entrance, they went in. But they did not find the body of the Lord Jesus...

Jesus: alive!

Luke 24:4-8 / Romans 5:17

- No body? Are you kidding? Well, maybe he wasn't really dead.

- What, you think the Romans can't tell when someone's dead? Do me a favour! They're the experts.

- Well, then, maybe the Jewish authorities took the body.

- Why on earth would they? And anyway, they'd say so straight away when these rumours started.

- I wonder if perhaps the disciples took his body?

- Let's face it, his 'devoted' followers were too scared even to be there for him when he was crucified. And some of them are putting their necks on the line now talking about these rumours: no-one would do that for a hoax.

- So, that leaves the rumours. Well, just maybe... after all, coming back from the dead is exactly what he said he'd do...

...they did not know what to think.

Suddenly two men in shining white clothes stood beside them. The women were afraid and bowed to the ground. But the men said, "Why are you looking in the place of the dead for someone who is alive? Jesus isn't here! He has been raised from death. Remember that while he was still in Galilee, he told you, 'The Son of Man will be handed over to sinners who will nail him to a cross. But three days later he will rise to life.'" Then they remembered what Jesus had said.

The devil couldn't stop him. Death couldn't keep him. The grave couldn't hold him. Check out the rest of Luke chapter 24 for occasions when Jesus visited people after his death. Jesus, the lord of life broke free! All the promises to his followers: life to the full, victory over death, life forever - vindicated! Jesus' identity as God in human flesh was proclaimed in the resurrection.

And we can be in on this:

Death ruled like a king because Adam had sinned. But that cannot compare with what Jesus Christ has done. God has been so kind to us, and he has accepted us because of Jesus. And so we will live and rule like kings.

Lord, thank you for your resurrection - and thank you that I can share in your resurrection life!

Who is He? • 37

Jesus: bursting out of the box

John 21:4-6, 12

Early the next morning Jesus stood on the shore, but the disciples did not realize who he was. Jesus shouted, "Friends, have you caught anything?"

"No!" they answered.

So he told them, "Let your net down on the right side of your boat, and you will catch some fish."

They did, and the net was so full of fish that they could not drag it up into the boat.

Jesus said, "Come and eat!" But none of the disciples dared ask who he was. They knew he was the Lord.

Jesus cooked fish. The most awesome things have happened: he's been crucified, laid in a tomb for three days, risen from the dead, astounding everyone, alive, triumphant, soon to take his throne in heaven, poised... And what he decides to do is hold a beach barbecue for his friends.

Maybe that's the scary thing: Jesus is involved in every aspect of our lives, no matter how everyday, how trivial.

We can try to put Jesus into some sort of spiritual box, just for Sundays, just for emergencies, just for special occasions, for times when we feel religious. We want a spiritual accessory, a bolt-on, while we carry on our lives as before.

Jesus won't have it. He wants in on every part of your life. Jesus cooks fish. He's with you when you're in the checkout queue, when you're fitting new wiper blades, when you're grumbling about your boss. It's a challenge. He wants all of your life and will change everything.

It's also a promise: that even the drab and tedious moments of our lives can be electrified by knowing his ever-presence.

Who is He?

Jesus: with you always

Matthew 28:20

I will be with you always, even until the end of the world.

And because of that, Jesus' kingdom is advancing. It's a far cry from old ladies crocheting doilies in draughty buildings. All around the world, Jesus' followers are fighting slavery, campaigning for justice, caring for AIDS sufferers, helping drug addicts, digging wells in drought areas. In Latin America and Africa there are places there has been such a work of God that crime has fallen, the jails stand empty, drug addiction is declining. Standing for truth and love in a world full of deception, injustice, selfishness and evil is the Kingdom advancing, in this world and the spiritual world.

In the Bible, Jesus is called the Lion of Judah. His followers are called to be like him: dangerous.

Jesus: our pattern

2 Corinthians 3:18 /
1 Corinthians 3:11

So our faces ... show the bright glory of the Lord, as the Lord's Spirit makes us more and more like our glorious Lord.

We need to take a good look at the real Jesus. Because if we choose to follow him, we will be transformed more and more into his likeness.

Who Is He? ★ 39

We will become more and more like God. What does that look like?

Jesus was confident and strong; kind but never a wimp; never insecure or inadequate; never cynical or pessimistic; respected by men, popular with women, loved by kids. He was free from anxiety, free from clutter. He knew how to make decisions, how to handle money, how to enjoy himself and how to control himself. He wasn't impatient, never lazy, or despairing, always able to cope. He dealt with criticism, was completely secure, was full of faith and hope. He reigned in life. That's what he offers us. What's our answer?

And Jesus is a team player. He didn't just gather a crowd of followers to wait on him. He picked a team, said he'd train them to be fishers of men, sent them out to proclaim good news, heal the sick, drive out demons. And that was just practice. Then he gave them the mission to take the message to the whole world.

He could have waved a finger. He could have sent angels. He chose to work with ordinary people. He still does. He's the coach and the manager and the captain. Jesus wants everyone to be part of the team, on the pitch. What sort of player are you? Listening, learning, playing to the game plan, getting out there? Ready? Or are you sitting around on the bench?

...Christ is the only foundation.

And he's given us the chance to take part in what he's building, this coming kingdom. Every word, every action that's centred in Jesus will endure forever. There's no such thing as an ordinary day when you walk with Jesus. Everything has the potential to be significant. The choice is ours.

Jesus: our hope

Revelation 21:1,3-5

I saw a new heaven and a new earth. The first heaven and the first earth had disappeared, and so had the sea.

I heard a loud voice shout from the throne: God's home is now with his people. He will live with them, and they will be his own. Yes, God will make his home among his people. He will wipe all tears from their eyes, and there will be no more death, suffering, crying, or pain. These things of the past are gone for ever. Then the one sitting on the throne said: I am making everything new. Write down what I have said. My words are true and can be trusted.

Take a look around. So much beauty and wonder in the world, so much that speaks of God. But so much that's a mess: destruction, pain, fear, hate. So much that's not as it's meant to be.

And take a glimpse into the future. What do you see? Nuclear war? Death by pollution? Chaos as the greenhouse effect changes the weather? A world filled with genetically modified humans? Global war, as Third World nations demand the return of the wealth the West has stolen from them?

Jesus is our hope. There is a day coming when he will return. In power and glory. It will be absolutely amazing! And he will put all things right, make everything perfect. With the real Jesus we can look to the future, whatever it brings, without fear. Ultimately the future is his.

Who is He? • 41

An invitation

If you would like to know more about what it means to be a Christian, you might like to complete this form and send it off to the CHRISTIAN ENQUIRY AGENCY. CEA, a charity supported by all the major churches, will put you in touch with Christians in your area - but no one will call on you or phone you unless you specifically ask them to.

If you don't want to cut this publication simply write the necessary details on a postcard or a piece of paper. No stamp is required if you post from a UK address.

CHRISTIAN ENQUIRY AGENCY (SU1)
FREEPOST SE 5940
London SE1 7YX

Please complete clearly in block capitals

I would like to know more about being a Christian:

Name: .... Address: ....

....

....

.... Postcode: ....

Please circle your age

16-20   21-30   31-40   41-60   60+

If you are under 16, please give your age: ....

Tick where appropriate

Yes, I would like some free literature ○

Yes, I would like a local Christian to contact me ○

by letter ○   by calling to see me ○

by phone ○   my number is ....

If you would like to give details of any previous church connections, please use this space:

....

This form can be photocopied

Feedback Welcome!

Scripture Union

SCRIPTURE UNION is a charitable organisation working around the world with the goal of making God's good news known to people of all ages, and encouraging them to meet God regularly through the Bible and prayer. As well as publishing books, Bible reading notes, and a range of church resources, Scripture Union produces videos and audio cassettes, works in schools, and runs holiday clubs and missions for children and young people.

If you'd like to give any feedback about *Bread for the Journey: the Identity series*, or find out more about any aspect of SU, you can:

- log on to http://www.scriptureunion.org.uk
- email info@scriptureunion.org.uk
- telephone 01908 856000
- write to Scripture Union at the address below.

Serving the King of Kings

CPO (Christian Publicity Organisation) is a literature mission, registered charity and professional design, print and distribution service. CPO provides...

- High quality, contemporary church publicity, evangelistic and discipleship resources through a mail order service and e-commerce. For a free catalogue call 01903 266400, or visit our website which has full details of our current catalogue and other services – www.cpo.org.uk

- A design, print and distribution facility that serves the Christian community – from the smallest local church to international charities – with state-of-the-art digital and conventional printing, warehousing and order fulfilment. For a free estimate call 01903 264556 and ask for our Print Sales Team. *'Bread for the Journey'* is designed and printed by CPO.

- 'Project Print', a fund supporting literature outreach in developing countries, which subsidises over six million items of print every year. For a leaflet giving further details, call 01903 266400.

If you do not receive regular information about CPO or SU please tick the relevant box below and return this form to the appropriate address.

❑ **Scripture Union**
   207-209 Queensway, Bletchley, Milton Keynes. MK2 2EB
   Tel: 01908 856000 Fax: 01908 856004
   Email: info@scriptureunion.org.uk

❑ **CPO**
   Garcia Estate, Canterbury Road, Worthing. BN13 1BW
   Tel: 01903 264556 Fax: 01903 830066
   Email: info@cpo.org.uk

MORE BREAD FOR THE JOURNEY

If you like what you've read so far, you might like to get the rest of the series. The coupon here will give you 50p off the cost of any of the other titles. Simply take it into your nearest Christian bookshop.

In case of difficulty in getting hold of Bread for the Journey telephone Scripture Union's mail order line on 01908 856006 or CPO on 01903 263354.

Addresses for both are given on page 43.

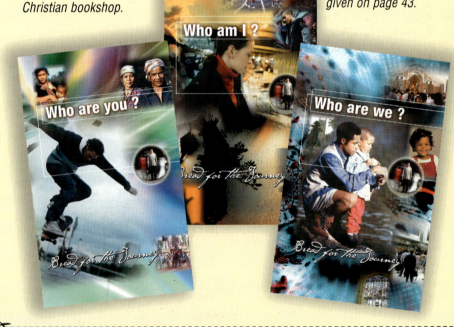

The bearer of this Voucher is entitled to a
Fifty pence reduction
in the purchase price of one other title in the Bread for the Journey: Identity series.

Name:

Address:

Shop stamp / details

Code: SUM

50p OFF

Bread for the Journey

Conditions: only one voucher per purchase. The voucher cannot be used with any other offer, or redeemed in part or in whole for cash. Photocopied coupons are not acceptable. Valid in the UK only until December 31, 2001.

To the retailer: To receive credit to your account, contact Customer Service Dept, STL, PO Box 300, Kingstown Broadway, Carlisle, Cumbria, CA3 0QS. Coupons must be received for redemption by January 31,